GROWING UP IN WINSLEY: MARILYN'S STORY

Hope you enjoy the read

Marilyn

Marilyn Maundrell

Ex Libris Press

Published in 2015
by Ex Libris Press
11 Regents Place
Bradford on Avon
Wiltshire   BA15 1ED

www-ex-librisbooks.co.uk

Printed by Print Essex

ISBN 978-1-906641-88-7

Acknowledgments

David and Barbara Feather for all their help
in the preparation of the manuscript and to
Winsley villagers for sharing their memories with
me. Please forgive any unintended errors.

CONTENTS

Winsley village scenes

The saddle-back tower of St Nicholas Church in distance

Reminiscing

This is the story of my life in the village of Winsley. I have so many, many memories which I feel I would like to pass on to the people who are still living there and to people living nearby, who may like to pass them on to others.

I still marvel at the fact that almost every turning you take in the village leads you to somewhere beautiful, with views across the valley and the fields where the local farmers kept their animals. The cricket field was always said to have the best views and setting for miles around. I used to go to a lot of the cricket matches when playing away. All were in lovely countryside but I absolutely believe in my own mind that Winsley Cricket Club was the best for miles around.

The old houses and cottages in Winsley too were so beautiful. (What am I talking about "were?". They still are!). There are lots still remaining and still lived in, but sadly not by locals. They are lovely people nevertheless. Prices rocketed, council houses were built, but I visit the local people still in their old houses today. I have been doing that and laughing and talking about the old times with my friends there.

Now I must get back to telling you about my life in the Seven Stars in Winsley.

My life in the village of Winsley was filled with many, many experiences – sad and heart-breaking ones, enjoyable and exciting ones. Looking back, they were character-building experiences. Most of the time I lived in the Seven Stars public house, together with my mother, father, granddad and grandma and, later on, my darling

Grandfather (second from right) with drinking companions in the yard outside the Seven Stars

My grandparetns: 'Grampy' and 'Nanny'

brother Terry (ten years younger than myself).

Having pondered about the past for many, many years, when I was out walking one day, I passed the Seven Stars, which was my home for so many years. I decided to sit on one of the seats in the yard at the front of the building and just reminisce. As I looked round, the memories came flooding back.

Well, I had been sitting a good hour but knew there were still many more memories waiting to be explored. Something told me to go on inside the pub and get a drink. As I approached the door, my eyes were drawn to the windows and I thought to look through them into the room beyond to try to recreate in my mind some of the scenes I had witnessed during my life in the pub. When I was young, you couldn't have looked through the windows because every one had net curtains. These curtains were so badly stained by the nicotine from the cigarette smoke that they became stiff and had to have separate tubs in the wash house. The anaglypta on the walls would also be stained brown and it was a hard job to rub it clean but my Mum used to do a good job getting everywhere clean on wash day.

Peering through the window, I could almost see in my mind's eye the shove ha'penny table which used to stand just underneath it. And then the fireplace, where the customers, especially the old men of the village, had sat and warmed themselves as they played cribbage, dominoes or shove ha'penny. What a lovely comforting background sound it had been for me, the murmur of village voices. Sometimes in the evenings when I was supposed to be in bed, I'd creep down and sit on the stairs, to see who was there and just listen to the customers talking amongst themselves about the football or cricket matches played the week before, swapping village gossip and banter, and sometimes suddenly exploding into laughter.

Above: Father, Mother and me

Mother, myself and brother Terry

The Seven Stars

I was born in 1936 at the Trowbridge Maternity Hospital and lived in Whiterow Park, Trowbridge, with my Mum and Dad. However, when I was two, we moved to The Seven Stars in Winsley. According to the Wiltshire Directory of 1920, my grandparents, Mr and Mrs H. Elms, were living at The Seven Stars and brought up their children there: my father, Leonard Elms and his two elder brothers, Percy and Leslie. By 1938, my grandparents, Kitty and Hubert Elms (Nanny and Grampy to me) had run the pub for many years but were now finding it too hard to manage on their own.

So my Mum and Dad, Kitty and Len Elms, (with me) had moved there to live with them. Their other sons, Percy and Leslie, had married and moved away by then. In addition, it turned out that my grandfather had been drinking a lot of the profits. This was confirmed later on, when my parents were reorganizing the garden and discovered a vast collection of empty beer and spirit bottles buried in an enormous rockery that my grandfather had made on the lawn behind the pub. As well as running the pub, my father continued working in the printing trade as manager of Sluggs in Trowbridge and then at Dotesios in Greenland Mills, Bradford-on-Avon as a rep.

My Mum suddenly had a new lifestyle which she regretted in the years to come, as she loved her and Dad's first house at Whiterow Park. I myself, of course, at the age of two did not have many memories of Whiterow Park.

As the years went by, when I was about seven or eight

years old, I had begun to notice more and more what was going on in the pub. The main pub, as most people who will read this will know, had the front door on the Winsley Road, where the buses passed through, and the side entrances were down in the car park. We used to call it the yard then. This yard was divided into two with big double gates by the side entrance of the pub as it is now, and that area right to the end of the land was filled with outhouses and two storeys of all different sorts of buildings.

I always thought the pub building absolutely wonderful. We had a big yard outside the back entrance with a huge tree growing in the centre. The middle of the tree had at one time or another been formed into an archway and a swing had been hung there. I taught my brother to ride his bicycle in the yard. The pub entrances were one at the front next to the old mounting block and one of the outer doors was down the yard on the side of the building, and to get there you had to cross the yard. The years when I was there, it was surrounded by outhouses of all descriptions.

These outbuildings were absolutely incredible, they gave me such fun during my life there. Inside it was all on different levels and the inside virtually went round in a circle, up one staircase, across a little landing, through a big oak door with different walls leading to different rooms and a little latch peg way to open them. Lo and behold, you look at the side of the wall and there was another door. You open this one, go down three steps and there was another room, and so it went on. There were about

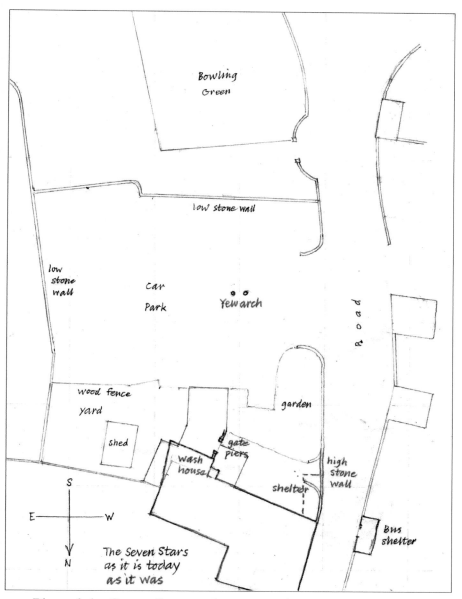

Plan of the Seven Stars and its grounds (Gareth Slater)

12 rooms I think altogether and there was one long room which you got to from the inside, which actually was on top of all the buildings in the yard. We called this the club room, mainly because the football club used it to clean themselves in the tin baths of water after the match had finished. Towels and tin baths of warm water were put there for them to use.

The pub had stone floors, with open fires in every room (no central heating in those days!), no bathroom, either, and two outside toilets shared with the customers – one for the men and one for the women. There were no flushing toilets, just the buckets to empty. Every bedroom had commodes standing next to the beds. Eventually, toilets were installed in the passageway leading to the back door.

The men of the village – small business owners, farmers and workmen – would stop work and turn up at around mid-day for their lunch and morning drink. Some would bring their bread and cheese into the bar and toast it on long toasting forks. Sometimes they would let me have a taste. Mum would have pickled onions and pickled eggs on the bar to sell. Tins of Smiths crisps were kept behind the bar. I have never tasted crisps like them, so crispy and a little oily.

When the brewery lorry came, they would roll the barrels down into the pub and into the cellars on long planks of wood they brought with them.

There was one very cosy wood-panelled room called the Snug and sometimes the Smoke Room, which was frequented by the councillors and businessmen to hold their meetings. I remember when, sometimes, I had to knock on the door and ask if I could walk through to get to the passage which led the way to the family kitchen and the stairway to the bedrooms (one bedroom leading off to another) and down steps. Then, when you had reached the last bedroom, you walked down another stairway, which came out in front of the bars – a big, heavy curtain hung across the entrance end of this lovely stairway.

There was a long room called the Tap Room. I think it was called the Tap Room because they used to tap the barrels in that area. It was the dart-playing area also. In the winter time, there was always a roaring fire burning there and one of the local old guys who had a long beard and loved his cider would pour his cider into a copper slipper and poke it into the embers to keep it warm. It was in the Tap Room that around the age of eight I would tap dance on the tables. The regulars would call out "Where's our little maid? When's she going to dance?" I would dance the Sailors' Hornpipe and Scottish dances (of a kind) and sometimes I was given a sixpence for my money box.

In the Tap Room, games of cards were played, dominoes, crib and shove ha'penny. Shove ha'penny fascinated me. Sometimes when the pub was closed, I used to go over to the table and have a game with some of my friends.

In some ways, the regulars were like my parents, looking after me and keeping me amused while my parents were working. Often the customers would ask me what I had done that day, especially Wing Commander Thomas from the Manor House, a friend of Dad's. He would ask me

Family and friends in the bar of the Seven Stars stopping off for a pint

The bar in the Seven Stars

how school was that day or had I been riding.

The Tap Room was frequented most Saturday nights by the cricketers or the footballers who had played their matches that afternoon. They would go home after the matches, change and then return with their wives to discuss the afternoon's play. The barrels were kept on trestles behind the bar, and underneath were small enamel dishes to catch the surplus beer which trickled down when the spills were put into the top of the barrel. I remember my brother (who was ten years younger than me) when he was little, about one or two years old, would move across the floor by tucking one leg under his bottom and pushing himself along with it. In this way, he was just the right height to discover the drip bowls and drink from them. The customers would roar with laughter as he propelled himself, faster and faster, from dish to dish. I think he took a very early liking to Usher's brews, although he never drank a lot in his adult life.

I remember how excited Terry got when Dad decided to have a fruit machine installed in the Tap Room – another way to keep the customers occupied and perhaps stay a little longer than usual. When the men came to empty the machines of the coins that had been inserted to make the machine work, they used their own special coins to service the machine and always gave him a handful of their coins for him to play with after they had gone. In the end, we didn't keep the machine too long as it was too noisy.

In the Smoke Room, or the Snug as it was often called, there was a bell on the wall which, when pressed, brought the people serving the drinks swiftly in to take the orders of spirits and beers, or crisps or fags. Very cosy it was, with a fireplace – a fire was always alight and glowing nicely when the weather was not too warm, making the room very cosy and snug. It would fascinate me watching them pick a spill out of a copper holder, light it from the fire, then light their pipes and throw the spill in the fire. The floor-to-ceiling wooden cupboards were each side of the fireplace, and the walls were wood-panelled half-way up, except the wall leading away from the door up the side-passage. This wall had stained glass windows running round the top. I used this room to do my homework. Sometimes, I had not finished when the first customers arrived. They always asked if I had a problem with my homework and helped me out. Another door in this room led to the entrance of the Jug and Bottle and the stone steps leading up to the pavement outside.

The Jug and Bottle was a tiny wee room, about four people could stand there and wait to be served through a little window which slid up and down. The Jug and Bottle was used a lot in the evenings; men and women would bring their jugs and stone bottles to be filled up and then take them home to drink. Crisps and fags, too, were usually taken home but – staff were very strict about who they handed the fags out to. In part of the yard by the back door, there were two open-fronted sheds with wooden tables and chairs arranged there. These were used a lot to enable small children to come with their parents and have their lemonade and crisps.

The cellar in the pub always housed fruit and veg of

A game of shove ha'penny

Father on one of his beloved motorcycles

some description from the garden, as well as the eggs from the chickens, and rabbits and pheasants that the gamekeepers of Conkwell Grange estate brought in for Mum to hang in the cellar. Mum's rabbit stews, I remember well – yum, yum!

There were little buildings in the yard for keeping the pet rabbits, cats and dogs and, in my mind's eye, I can see where the old wash-house used to be. The washing was done there using a very old stone boiler built into the wall with the fireplace underneath which my grandfather used to light up very early every Monday morning. Tin baths were placed along settles around the building, into which was poured the warm water which was used for swilling the clothes out. The clothes were swilled around using an old wooden pole. One bath was reserved for blue-bagging the whites. A little blue cube, a Reckitt cube, just a little bigger than the cube used to chalk the end of a snooker cue, was dissolved into the water and brightened the whites once they had been washed and swilled. Net curtains were washed frequently and separately because of the nicotine that constantly stained them.

Finally, the clothes were lifted out and put through the mangle, which was placed over a drain in the middle of the stone floor. This must have been a very hard job, considering the weight of the clothes, as we could hardly turn the mangle handle around. Once mangled, the clothes were ready to be pegged out on the washing line in the garden.

We had a big range in the kitchen and, on bath nights, tin baths were placed on the floor and filled with lovely warm water. Towels were hung over the oven door rails attached to the front of the range. In the winter time, the oil lamps were lit and it was so cosy. After a while, rubbed and dried with the lovely, warm towels, I would put on my nightdress and up the wooden stairs I went to bed. I used to lie in bed listening to customers in the bars talking and occasionally singing. As I mentioned before, sometimes I used to sneak down the stairs, hide behind the curtains at the bottom and watch and listen to the banter of the customers.

On the far side of the yard, which was walled, there was a beautiful grotto stone archway leading to a lovely garden with a large lawn with its rockery, fruit trees and vegetables, all the fruit and veg you could think of. A path led to a gate which led you to the pig sties and a small paddock where calves were kept. There was another fantastic building in it – the Granary, which housed the chickens when our family lived there. Stone steps ran up the side of this building and at the top was a little doorway. Through the doorway, you could see an agricultural machine, possibly a threshing machine for separating out the corn from the chaff. This corn was used to feed the chickens, which were kept in the space below. It was my job to collect the eggs from the nest boxes every day and to feed them every night. My big dread – and you could bet your bottom dollar it would come true – was that the rats would leap out at me when I slid open the lids.

Close by the chicken house, was a mini orchard filled with fruit trees and bushes with various sweet fruits. We also grew all the vegetables we would need for the family.

In the wall to the right was a large double gateway leading out into the road which would be opened wide enough to allow lorries and vans in to collect chickens and pigs and now and then a few calves to be transported to Trowbridge Monday Market. As you walked further down the paddock you would come across the pigsties.

Something I forgot to mention when describing the upstairs rooms at the Seven Stars was a door in the Games Room (the same rooms where the footballers used to wash themselves down after the football matches had finished). It was also where the kids in the village used to play when it was pouring with rain. They were very lucky to have this area.

As you opened the door, a long room stretched out before you with windows looking out onto the ground of 'Bleak House', a house just down the road to the right as you walked out from the pub. At the bottom of this room, on the wall, there were several glass cabinets displaying various wildlife animals, which had been killed, stuffed and mounted, and in the centre of the wall, a large stag's head was also displayed. I didn't enjoy looking at them.

Then along, a bit to the right, there was a smallish wooden door set high up in the wall. It was just big enough for me to enter by standing on a chair and I was able to have a look at what was inside. One day, I noticed a stack of oil paintings leaning against the wall, mostly country scenes and portraits. I used to dream that one day I would discover something really valuable. There were tiny pieces of furniture as well.

Mum was always anxious when I went into this 'hidden

room', as I used to call it, because in parts, the floorboards were rotting, but if you were careful, it was OK. This room was actually on top of the outhouses running up the side of the yard. One of them was the wash-house, of which I have described earlier. The ceiling of the wash-house was the floor of the hidden room. The other outhouses used to house various small animals.

I did hear however, that one of the previous landlords, when he left, took several interesting and old things with him. (All above board, we were led to believe.) I only wish that I had got there before him. There, that was quite interesting, wasn't it?

My own personal horror story

I must have been about 12 years of age, when one day after I had gone to the chicken houses, which were situated in the paddock, to clear the nest boxes of eggs and take them up to the pub. I heard the sound of boys' voices and laughter and at the same time a lot of squeaking and squealing. As I walked up through the garden, the squealing got louder and louder and I could hear the boys voices and laughter getting louder and sounding very excited but not in a very nice way. It sounded as if something horrible was happening. I ran towards the place where I thought the noise was coming from and there before my eyes was the most awful scene I had ever seen. Boys from the village had followed me down to the paddock near the chicken houses, caught a hen, and had taken it back up to the garden, tied it to a tree and were beating the poor thing to death with sticks. I screamed out for my grandpa – he was working on the vegetable plot – to come quickly. He came rushing. His language to the group of boys was not repeatable. He released the poor bird but alas its injuries were too severe and it died. I thought I was going to pass out. I cried and cried and cried. The boys were taken up to the pub, their parents contacted and told what had happened. The local copper was informed and told them to come to the pub immediately. He told the parents how serious this incident was and left them to punish them as they saw fit. He knew the parents and how upset and disgusted by the boys' behaviour they would be and could depend on them giving them a punishment they would not forget in hurry. I couldn't sleep for weeks. How could anyone be so cruel? From then on children were no longer allowed to play in the paddock when the animals were left unattended.

The envelope survived

The Seven Stars originally had a thatched roof, but this was destroyed by a fire in 1928 and the thatch was never replaced. While repairs and alterations were being done in the roof space, an envelope was found, badly scorched, with a message written on a piece of paper saying my grandparents had put a penny coin in an envelope and left it there. It survived, believe it or not, and I have to this day kept this precious note, handwritten by my grandparents, in two halves and very tattered and scorched with the date on.

More of my family

My father was born with a 'club foot' considerably shorter than the other. He wore leg irons, as they were then called, and were fitted to his boot and helped support his leg. He couldn't of course play any physical sports, so he concentrated on snooker, billiards, darts and bowls, playing bowls for many local village teams as well as Winsley. He did very well with all these games and won many cups, both singly and as part of a team, and eventually he played for the County. When his disability stopped him from joining the army, he consequently joined the Home Guard, the motor cycle section. He was always very keen on motorcycles and had several of them before he was married to Mum. Come to think of it, I think he had rather a good motorcycle when he first met my Mum and then when he became landlord of the Seven Stars he had two motorcycles as well. Mum and Dad loved the joy of riding them in the countryside; in those days no helmets of course, a lovely feeling with the wind blowing through your hair.

My Uncle, David Allsopp, my Mother's brother, was involved in the war. Apparently, while he was in Germany, immediately after the war, he was billeted with a German family. He fell in love with the daughter of the family but was very upset when he had to leave her behind. I don't know a lot of the detail, but for many years afterwards, every hour he would talk about the war. Any conversation would always go back to the war.

I remember the smell of my uncle's clothes when he used to come home from working in the factory, the smell of rubber. The smell was atrocious so we said "You can't come into the kitchen, you put your clothes in the stable. You leave them there and come on in after you have changed your clothes" and he used to go and hang them by the kitchen where we had double doors leading out from the kitchen. There was a hook to hang his clothes, like his jacket and his over-trousers. The smell of the rubber, how it used to linger on clothes.

As we were surrounded by farms, several of my relations were farmers locally and we had two or three farms in the neighbourhood.

Nanny Allsopp, my Mother's mother, used to cycle from Farleigh Wick to Winsley to help Mum with the daily chores. Two women, also from the village, used also to help Mum with the chores, for example, polishing or scrubbing the floors, whichever was appropriate; throwing out the old ashes of the five fireplaces and relighting, ready for opening at 11 a.m. This was a very important job, as the pub was a rambling building and fires were kept going in the winter time throughout the day.

I remember my Mother often reading this poem to me in our kitchen at The Seven Stars:

Memories of my Granny's Kitchen

My Granny in a big white apron,
Kitchen table, scrubbed and clean,
Delicious smells of eggs and bacon,
The biggest eggs I've ever seen.

Kitchen range, ashine with black lead,
Big old fender, made of brass,
Home-made rug of rags and canvas,
Cornflowers in a pewter vase.

There were gas lights hanging from the ceiling,
Casting shadows on the wall,
What a warm and cosy feeling,
With shutters closed as evening falls.

There were old stone jars of jams and gingers,
Standing on the middle shelf,
I'd climb a chair and crook my finger,
Lift the lid and help myself.

These are memories I treasure,
Memories of my childhood days,
The picture of my Granny's kitchen will hang
within my mind always.

(I always assumed this kitchen *was* our's at The Seven
Stars, Winsley.)

Nanny Allsopp rode a bicycle with a basket on the
front in which she would put some coal to take home for
her fire. Very sadly one day, when cycling home down the
hill past the Police Station, she cycled over a rough bit of
road – some coal fell out of the basket into the spokes of
the front wheel, causing her to crash, and she fell onto
the road into the path of the Bath bus coming up the hill
into the village. She was killed instantly and so, very,

very sadly, my mother was in that bus, returning from Trowbridge after collecting my brother from school. My mother suffered greatly for months, if not years, feeling guilty, seeing that Granny had been working hard that day doing some cleaning etc. at the pub. As far as I can remember, I was about ten when this happened.

Village leisure

Next to the Seven Stars, on the left, there was a bowling green donated by the brewery for use by the villagers. A bowling club was formed and bowling became so popular. Later on, the villagers asked for two more rinks to be laid, which was agreed upon. The club prospered and still thrives today, in the same place, near the Village Hall. A large shed close by served as the changing rooms and a committee meeting room.

The Village Hall was on the left of the pub paddock with an entrance with steps leading down to the road near the Manor House. It was very well equipped for its time, with a stage, changing rooms and courts set out for badminton. There were gardening clubs, plays, pantos, concerts, girl guides; all the many and various activities which made up village life and at the bottom of the hall there was a little kitchen and doors leading to the outside. This badminton club still exists, as do many of the other village activities. Many, many people would remember the famous sausage and mash and baked beans suppers served there at the end of the season (spuds provided by the well known farmers, the Daniels family in Turleigh).

The yard at the side of the pub was a very handy area for the steam roller man when he was tarring the road. He would pull in, as would many of the village workers, to take his morning break and buy refreshments from my mother, who supplied the usual bread, cheese, pickle and crisps.

Terry Elms, my brother, played cricket for Winsley for several years. He loved it and made lots of friends. I occasionally used to watch the home matches. Sometimes, as I walked down the lane towards the cricket field, I would hear the cricket ball make contact with the bat, somehow that was a lovely sound to me – welcoming you down to see the match. If they were lucky enough to score a run or runs, a loud cheer could be heard and clapping of hands. On a lovely sunny day, it was very nice to be participating in supporting your village team while sipping a lemonade.

Terry's wife, Jean, and their children became very interested in the Cricket Club too. She used to help with the cricket teas and sometimes their older girls helped as well.

Once a week the portable cinema picture van would pull in at the pub and its doors would open to reveal the cinema screen inside. The villagers would gather in the yard to stand and watch the films, black and white, of course. They also had to stand throughout the performance. A fish and chip van visited every Friday and villages queued for their fish and chips.

We played lots of games in the village, especially down at the playing field, which was situated near the War

The Bowls Club

Memorial. 'Fox and Hounds' was very popular, as long as we got rid of the white chalk marks from the road fairly soon afterwards. I'm afraid the playing field was acquired by a local builder, Phil Beaven, and he built a large house there for himself and his family. As far as I can remember, Miss Knatchbull from the Manor let Mr Bevan acquire the piece of land in question.

Badminton in the Village Hall

The children from the village missed having the playing field. It didn't have a lot in it. There was a see-saw and swings and wooden seats. It had quite a large area of grass which enabled us to play bat and ball and leapfrog, kick a ball around and sit on the seats and chatter. Perhaps we would eat some crisps and drink lemonade, which was purchased from the pub. It was a very long time before the village had another playing field – in fact I think it was when the new school was built in the late seventies.

There were lots of things you could do to entertain yourselves in the village. One of my friends would come and stay with me at the pub and we would catch the train to Bath – known as the 'Midnight Rocker' – and spend the day there (steam trains in those days, great fun). I loved travelling on them, but had to remember not to open the windows because of the smut coming from the engine. We travelled from Avoncliff station, through Freshford and Limpley Stoke. We walked to the station from Winsley, down through the fields; cows were usually grazing in the fields. This proved a bit tricky when we returned home later, especially if it was dark. We took a torch to use when we came home if it was dark, but occasionally bumped into a cow or two. I remember saying to the cows, sorry, which caused my friends and I to laugh lots as we walked across the fields to home.

When we did come home from Bath and pulled into Avoncliff station, an announcement was made for anyone getting off the train to please move to the front of the train so we could get off the train on to the platform, which wasn't very long. Then off up the fields we went and when we got to the pub, the customers would make sure Dad was distracted so we could get in without him seeing how late it was.

We could also swim in the river; Warleigh weirs was a popular place to go, or we could swim in the old Baths at

Bradford-on-Avon, where these were sometimes covered with boards for us to dance – I remember this quite well. The village hall in Winsley also, very often, had something going on; some of the boys in the village had set up small bands where they performed here. This attracted the others kids in the village to go.

Many of the richer people who lived in the village had their own private tennis courts and if you asked nicely, they would let you play an occasional game of tennis with friends. One family especially, who I knew quite well, lived along the top road by the name of Mr and Mrs Carlisle. Mrs Carlisle would let a few of us play tennis on the court in their garden. She would bring us cold drinks and sometimes stopped to watch us play. One of her sons (Michael) belonged to the badminton club which was in the village hall in the grounds of the Seven Stars.

There were heaters along one side of the room, which was a bit awkward when you ran to return a shuttlecock that was coming down the side line, and I seem to remember that the walls were of asbestos. Michael Carlisle went for a shot once, fell against the wall and broke several of the asbestos sheets.

The hall roof was very low and visiting teams, who usually played in sports centres with very high roofs, found this irritating, not having many opportunities for hitting the shuttles up high and to the back of the court. We of course played a lot of net shots and this annoyed them as they had to play a very fast game, but we had tremendous fun.

I remember that a Miss Knatchbull, who ran an

Dinner in the Village Hall

Village children in a fancy dress parade

The village hall played host to a variety of events

ambulance car service, used this car to drive us to our away matches. She very often came over to the hall when we had our home matches, from just over the road from Winsley Manor where she lived, to watch us play. She sat up on the stage and watched the matches from there. All the refreshments for the end of the match were put on plates on tables on the stage and we used to have to watch Miss Knatchbull very carefully; I think she loved the refreshments more than watching the game and she would eat a large proportion of them if we weren't careful. She was a lovely lady really, a real character.

I helped to run the club for quite a long time; we had a lot of members and at the end of season we had a sausage and mash and baked bean supper. Potatoes and sausages were supplied by the local farmers who were members of the club. Supper was prepared in a tiny little kitchen at the end of the hall which is still there today being used, slightly modernised though!

The garden club held a village flower show. Local bands came now and then for gigs. My brother sometimes played the drums on these occasions. There was a Reading Room for quiet reading, as the name suggests, but it was also used for billiards and snooker.

Brownies met in a hall in Turleigh and there were junior football teams. For the older ones there was a Young Farmers Club and a Young Conservative Club.

Sometimes, during the Summer months, kids from Bradford-on-Avon would cycle up the hill to Winsley and 'hang around' near the bus shelter or sit on the wall of the village school, waiting to see if anyone from the village

The village reading room on the left which housed the billiards club

'was coming out to play'. They would then while away a couple of hours or so, exchanging news of what they had all been doing recently. Mr Eales, the Headmaster of the school, used to shout at anyone who sat on the wall, as this wall surrounded the school playground and the thought of anyone jumping over the wall and getting through the small hedge and onto the playground worried him.

During these gatherings of young people, visits were made to the 'Jug and Bottle' in the Seven Stars and crisps and various drinks were purchased. Those were usually consumed in the bus shelter or in the wooden shelters in the pub yard.

One day when we were meeting in the bus shelter, swapping all our news, one girl asked me how the new boyfriend was; how far did he go? Well, I was so cross – so served her right, as I responded with "Oh, a few more buttons were undone. I'll leave what followed to your imagination" was my cheeky reply. Honestly, my interest in the lads was doing things together – (for the benefit of the readers – no not that!) in climbing trees, swinging on the ropes, swimming in the river. I was such a tomboy. I also loved going to the pictures down town to the Alexander Cinema. I loved the pictures. Sometimes, for a change, we went to the Gaumont cinema in Trowbridge.

Another thing I loved to do when out walking with my dog across the fields on a lovely sunny afternoon was to lie down on the grass and watch the clouds scudding across the sky forming shapes which in one's imagination could be all sorts of things and, gosh, how about the unbelievable colours in the sunsets and sunrises. I used to get quite emotional with the sheer beauty of it all. Even now, when I'm all grown up (!!), I love to take the bus to Bath just to look at the views and the skies, as we travel from Winsley down Winsley Hill and on to Bath. What a beautiful area we live in.

Village people

PC Ford lived down the hill in the police house opposite the war memorial. He used to do a patrol of the village in the evenings to make sure the youngsters were behaving themselves. Some of us used to meet in the bus shelter and I had a little sweetheart in the village. I was about 14 or 15 years old and I used to meet him there. My Mum and Dad used to send me to bed and meanwhile my friends, including my 'special' friend, would be gathering in the bus shelter having kissing contests. I was told not to join them as it was getting quite late, but I used to climb out of the window, down on to the wooden shed roof below, and then down onto the street to join them, including my sweetheart as I didn't want to miss out. If PC Ford was on his rounds, he would say "Marilyn Elms, you in there?" (He was a friendly policeman and my Dad had asked him to look out for me.) "Your Dad wouldn't want you to be staying out too late." I used to hide the cigarettes that I pinched from the shelf behind the bar to give to my lovely Geoff.

Sunday mornings, I had piano lessons given to me by a Mr Cumley from Bradford-on-Avon. He would drive up the hill and come into the yard, leave his elderly mother and the dog in the pub with plenty to drink, then I would go upstairs to our lounge, where the piano was, for my lesson. One thing I remember well was that he used to suck his teeth a lot – very off-putting when I was trying to hear what he was saying. There was another piano teacher in the village living in a cottage near the village hall, by the name of Mrs Withy, a much better teacher I thought. I later continued my lessons when I was sent away to boarding school near Bridgwater in Somerset.

Dirty Sam, as he was known, was sitting in the bus shelter looking a bit anxious, as no-one had stopped to buy his wares. He would sell his bits and pieces – cottons, buttons, razor blades, shoe polish, candles, etc., etc. – from a cardboard tray which hung around his neck. The children were very frightened of him as his face was always black and scary (this was the result of him being gassed in the war time) and his clothes rather shabby. I told the children why the marks were on his face and from then on he was their friend, telling them many stories about the war. Gradually, his shabby appearance didn't matter any more. You couldn't help staring at him; there would always be something to get your attention – worn out shoes, dirty jacket – but then he always waved to the children as he got up and walked away. Their scary man became their friend; he was certainly mine.

Harry Scadding, who lived in the village, ran a little hair cutting business from a wooden shed at the bottom of his garden. Anyone and everyone used to visit his shed – for a shave (men only of course) and the children and their mums went for hair cuts. These usually took place, I remember, on Sunday mornings. I used to go and have my hair cut there. The little shed used to fascinate me. I remember he had all the necessary tools laid out ready to use: scissors, shaving brushes, combs, shaving cream and aftershave. There was a mirror on the wall in front and a hand mirror to show the customers the back of the head. A leather strop hung from a hook on the wall to sharpen the razors. Mr Scadding's 'proper' job, for want of a better description, was at H. J. Knee's Garage in Trowbridge where he worked for many years, and where they dealt with cars. He was a friend of Dad's; a nice man and was involved a lot in what went on in the village.

Percy and Marge Hazel used to live at The Chase, a big beautiful house situated on the left hand side of the road leading down to the Winsley cricket field. Percy cared for a few cows in a field near the house and the milk was taken to a small dairy built onto the side of The Chase. Very often I took a container and bought milk to take back to the pub for Mum.

Margery Beale lived in a lovely cottage in the village of Winsley with her husband Gordon. I first knew her when she lived in Murhill and she used to play badminton in Winsley Village Hall. Also, we were both volunteers at the Bradford-on-Avon Music Centre. Unfortunately, she was taken ill with cancer and had to give up the volunteering. We met up again when one day I was on the way home after walking 'Jo', my black labrador, and was passing her cottage – Gordon was working in the garden. (You never knew what he would be working on; he never seemed to finish anything for a long time after starting the jobs.) We very often used to have a chat and on this day, I asked him how Margery was and he replied "resting, but I'm sure she would love to see you and Jo, so come on in. Mind the garden gate; its a bit wobbly – needs a bit of attention. I'll be in soon and I'll make us a cup of tea." So, in we went; Jo made himself comfy on the rug in front of the fire. I could see that Margery was not too well; she told me she had been to hospital that morning for some treatment for her cancer but she said "Sit down and tell me your news." These get-togethers went on for quite a few months.

On her better days, she would play a tune or two on the piano and sometimes, I would play a tune, or try to!! Compared with Margery's playing, mine was rubbish. We laughed a lot about that. She would say "Marilyn, I'll have to give you some lessons." She was a very accomplished piano player.

Well, I did so much enjoy my visits to see her and Gordon. He would not stay in with us very long. "Must go and get on." He would say "don't bother with the washing up, I'll do it later. I've put a bowl of water down on the floor in the kitchen with a biscuit for Jo."

Unfortunately, Margery, after a long brave battle, died. I went to her funeral to say my goodbyes. I have lovely memories of our chats. A lovely lady.

Now, I have an amusing tale to tell involving Colonel Walker, who lived in Burghope Manor. When I was 15 or 16, he had his grandsons to stay in the school summer holidays and, during this time, I took them round the lanes with their pony. Then they took it in turns to ride her. The boys not riding took their bicycles. After we had had enough riding, we went back to the Manor and I took the pony to her stable, rubbed her down, locked the stable door and went home for lunch.

Well, there I was eating my lunch with Mum and Dad when the phone rang. Dad answered it and even from where I was sitting, I heard the Colonel shouting down the line, "Leonard (that being my Dad), get that daughter of yours back round here immediately, she forgot to shut the stable door properly; the pony has got out and played havoc with the front lawns. Clumps of grass and earth everywhere. I've got a ruddy croquet match tonight with friends and the lawn's a mess."

So back round I went and the Colonel's housekeeper's son was there looking just a little bit perturbed. He was home on leave from the Air Force and had seen me go into the stables and came round to say 'hello' and have a little cuddle. I hadn't seen him for months and had got distracted. Thus the stable door was not closed properly. So, down on our hands and knees we got and patted these little clods of grass and earth back into the lawn. It took ages, hours in fact. Later that afternoon, the Colonel rang home again. Dad answered the phone and called out to me saying, "Lucky for you, the lawn isn't too bad at all. The match will be going ahead." I was worried that the Colonel might stop me from taking the boys out for their rides but the croquet match went off all right and he was jolly decent about it all and things went on as usual. Phew!

Cyril Organ was the blacksmith when I was living in Winsley and his forge was just over the road from the Seven Stars. I used to love going across to watch him shoe the horses and make all sorts of tools. I imagine that the local farmers used to keep him busy, either forging new tools, or mending broken ones, making hoops for children to play with in the streets where there was not much traffic. Over the years, there were quite a lot of blacksmiths in Winsley.

Winsley Garage, along the Top Road, was owned by Mr and Mrs Little who had a daughter named Nina. This garage was originally the bungalow where they lived, built mainly from asbestos. It was gradually altered. A shop and petrol pumps were added and workshops built alongside. Men from the village used to drive the different cars and buses that were booked to go to various places; shows in Bristol for instance and London. Mr Kettlety, the chauffeur from Winsley House sometimes helped out with the driving, complete with uniform. It became a thriving business for many years.

I have already talked about my horse-riding days in Winsley and the surrounding countryside, and I was lucky enough to make friends with Jean Titley who lived with her Mum and Dad and brother in a bungalow in Ashley Lane. The family had moved up the hill from Bradford-on-Avon. Her father had kept a jewellers' shop in the town and they lived in a flat above the shop for several years but he still ran it after they moved to Winsley. Mrs Titley was very kind to me. She let me have some of Jean's riding clothes. She was a dressmaker and a few

*Car from
Winsley
Manor,
1924*

Winsley Garage

*Bus used
for village
outings*

dresses came my way as well.

Jean loved riding so we got on very well, riding out in the fields and around the lanes and, what a coincidence, the horses she rode and took hunting belonged to my husband-to-be's uncle – Johnny Maundrell.

Johnny Maundrell was a plumber, but when war broke out he joined the Royal Engineers. When he was about 14 years of age he had joined the Crusaders' Boys Club where he was interested in the boxing. So in his time, he had become quite a good boxer, winning numerous trophies. He was lightweight champion of Wiltshire. However, during the war, he lost fingers as a girder had fallen on his fingers when they were building a Bailey bridge, so his boxing days were over.

Ronald Huntley was a friend of my brother's, who used to play in the Games Room at the pub, as quite a lot of the village children did, if it was pouring down outside. It must have been when they were about eight or nine years of age.

Ronald and his sister Noreen lived with their Mother and Father in a cottage next to the Wheatsheaf, formerly a shop, in the village. His father was very interested in model railways and had tracks mounted on tables which ran throughout the attic rooms – Noreen took me up to look at this set-up – it was amusing. There were various different engines, lots of carriages, a ticket office, and lots of wagons for taking heavy goods to various destinations, and signals. There was also a little model of the station master and guard with his flags, luggage and trolleys for carrying the luggage. I could go on forever I'm sure, if my memory was better.

When Ronald was older, you would, if you lived in this area, often see him flying his microlight aircraft, a Dragon 150, sometimes on his own; other times with a passenger on board. But, unfortunately one day, with his friend's wife on board, Mrs Fry from the Riding Stables at Widbrook Farm, he crashed in the Southway Park area. No one was seriously hurt, but afterwards, he decided 'that was a bit close' and gave up flying himself, but I expect he kept his interest going – if only by watching other people fly.

Ronald's sister, Noreen, who had married a local farmer, Roger Silcox from Pottick's Farm, started a new venture at Conkwell – a clay pigeon shooting business which I think became very popular. Noreen took me to look at the set-up. It seemed to me quite impressive and I believe it was a very successful business. Nevertheless, they moved on to farm elsewhere after a while.

Joyce Edmunds' parents used to run the Sunnyside Nurseries in the village. She was often seen on the buses, always knitting away, always sitting in the same seat and chatting away to her friend, the bus conductor, and the locals who were on the bus. Mum, whenever she needed some fresh flowers, would pop down the road to buy them from the Nurseries. I would sometimes go and help choose them with either Mr or Mrs Edmunds.

Tom Bowles of Hartley Farm runs the Hartley Farm Shop and the Bowles family has expanded it enormously. Each generation has taken to farming at Winsley and all the farming land around for several miles. I first knew the Bowles' family when Bert Bowles lived on Church Farm with his Mother and Father, a brother John, and sisters Matty and Mary. Unfortunately, John met with an accident at Church Farm when he was 18 years of age. He was run over by one of their tractors. The brakes had slipped, he fell out and suffered a fatal head injury. Mr Godwin, who worked on the farm, was on the tractor with him. A lovely farming generation after generation who seem to be farming everywhere around the lanes.

The three Bowles family children

More horsey antics

Sometimes my friends with horses would trot in to say hello or to ask me to exercise their horses for them when they returned to school. There was a mounting block at the front of the pub which in the early days was used a lot, but as the traffic increased, it wasn't a safe place any more. I got to know the people from the grand houses around by offering to exercise their horses while the children were away at boarding school. It was through Mr Brooks of Conkwell Grange that I met Susan Milburn, the daughter of Sir Eric Milburn, and arrangements were made for me to exercise her horse. I considered myself very lucky to be able to ride horses free of charge. I learned to ride under the supervision of a young woman, Joan Griffiths, who stayed for periods at Winsley Manor.

Jean Titley (left) and myself on horseback

One day, I was exercising a lovely chestnut horse called Sunshine in one of the fields that was situated along the side of the road that ran along the side of Limpley Stoke Hill. On this particular day, I was out going down through the avenue of trees that also ran down the hill when the double-decker bus went by. The locals were used to seeing me in the field with the horses and on this particular morning they were waving out, being nice and friendly and the driver of the double-decker bus wanted to join in with his 'hello', if that's what you want to call it. He put his finger on the horn and peeped at me. Well, this spooked the horse and it bolted. Oh, I was petrified. It went right down through the middle of the avenue of trees and I had to quickly put my legs round the horse's neck to stop me getting entangled in the branches of the trees. Anyway, eventually she stopped and we went back to the stables. Was I scared!

Shopping in the village

In the old village of Winsley, there were two shops. The Post Office/General Store and the Wheatsheaf were the only two places where one could do a little bit of general shopping. The Co-op butchery van from Bradford-on-Avon would drive up the hill with a collection of meat for the villagers to buy. Also Bryant's shop van from Bradford-on-Avon visited Winsley with various household items for sale, including oil. Oil lamps were used a lot in the village when our family lived there, also candles were available from the van. The Fish van was also a very popular visitor in the village, selling a large selection of fish and, of course, we mustn't forget the Fish and Chip van. So you see, although the village had only two shops, it was able to purchase eggs and vegetables from the farmers and, of course, 'Dig for Victory' encouraged anyone who had a bit of land at their disposal to grow their own fruit and vegetables.

The village shop, known as the Wheatsheaf

Watercress gardens were close at hand and during the summer time, Mr and Mrs Holly from Murhill grew and sold their strawberries from their 'Strawberry Gardens'. Milk, I used to collect from the Dairy at 'The Chase' where Percy and Marge Hazel were living, as herdsman and housekeeper respectively. Cattle grazed in the fields nearby overlooking the valley. The owners of The Chase were Mr and Mrs Harvey. This house was situated at the side of the road leading down to the cricket ground, surrounded by fields and amazing views of the valleys all around.

Winsley cricket team gather in front of the pavilion

The Post Office was in the middle of the village. I had a savings account there and I still have my savings book. Mr and Mrs Gerrish ran this little shop; it served as a shop, where the villagers could purchase many useful items, groceries and lots of useful things for the home.

There were many wells in the village. There was a wonderful circular stone one in the grounds of the Winsley Manor and another one underneath the bus shelter.

Market Day in Trowbridge

Market day in Trowbridge was always on a Tuesday. This was one of my favourite outings with my grandfather. Sometimes, my grandmother's sister, Aunt Rose, who farmed in North Bradley, would come with us. Then, when we had done all we wanted to do at the Market, we would go back home to the pub for lunch. Mum would always make a junket for dessert. It was their favourite, but horrible, I thought!

I almost forgot to tell you a couple of things – two more treats from my grandfather. If it was time to replace some of our chickens with new stock, he would buy me a box of baby chicks. You know the ones I mean, the boxes with the circles cut out. The chicks were gorgeous. They would peer at me through the holes, chirping away like mad. I adored those fluffy chicks, they always smelt so lovely. I just wanted to cuddle them. They had a certain warm and fluffy smell about them. When we got home after the market, Grampy would let some of the chicks out onto the kitchen table to allow me to pick them up. Then I would take them all to the chicken house down in the paddock.

We usually kept about 30 to 40 chickens. The nest boxes were arranged all around the bottom half of an old outhouse. Containers for the grain were against one of the walls and, if I was around, my job was to feed and water them. With them safely delivered to their nesting boxes and the metal containers containing their food all put ready for me to give them their supper later on. This was a job I didn't really care for much, because when I slid the lids across to get to the food, rats would very often jump out.

We did also have a very, very bad-tempered cockerel, and handsome and beautiful as he was, he would spend most of his time in the fruit trees and if anyone passed underneath those branches, beware! Your hair would no longer be looking as it should. He would fly down and perch on your head.

The other treat was – Grampy used to keep a pin in his lapel on his jacket. This was to enable me to hook my favourite treat out of their shells – a bag of whelks in vinegar from Trowbridge Market, in a long paper bag.

Visits to the Murhill caves

Murhill caves were one of the favourite places where the Winsley children would explore. We took candles which we lit and entered the caves. We would eat the refreshments we had taken with us and just talked and laughed about each other's bit of news, about what had happened at school that day and what films we had seen at the cinema, etc., etc.

Strawberries at Murhill

Mr and Mrs Holly had a cottage in Murhill and some of their land was turned into a patch planted with strawberries. These were picked and one could buy them – delicious! It was very pleasant to mingle with the locals as they picked their strawberries, admiring the view down the Limpley

Stoke valley. One had to be sure you had wiped your mouth round. As is the usual thing to do, you had eaten quite a few strawberries as you walked around, denting Mr and Mrs Holly's profits. As usual the children ate more than they put in their containers.

The views across the Limpley Stoke valley are absolutely fantastic. I still like to travel to Bath either on the bus or the train, just to take in the wonderful countryside.

Other childhood activities

Conkwell Woods were another place to explore. We tied ropes to the trees, swinging on them and daring each other to jump. There were little farms dotted around with lots of animals to be seen – cattle, sheep, horses and what we loved to see were the baby piglets dashing around and squealing. They looked so pretty with their little plump bodies and bottoms, with curly tails.

Lambing time was wonderful with the young lambs playing in the fields. There was usually lots to be seen in the fields running down the side of Winsley Hill.

At Turleigh, a little hamlet just down a path near Winsley war memorial, you could see the Turleigh 'trows'. This was an enclosed stone gulley along which fresh spring water flowed. It still does to this day. There were watercress beds on land belonging to a cottage just behind the trows and the cress was sold from this cottage. We used to knock the door and ask if there was any for sale. Mum used to make us lovely watercress sandwiches for tea, just with a little salt added. On hot Summer days, I remember soaking my feet in the water on my way back home, after going for a walk around the lanes. Our dog used to enjoy drinking the wonderful cold water while paddling behind to cool his feet.

When the apples were ripe on the trees in the gardens behind us, many fell to the ground so we would make sure that there was a big bag in our pockets to pick up the fallers, to take home. This was not exactly scrumping as they had fallen by the wayside.

Transport

We were lucky to have a good bus service in Winsley running at the same time! One bus ran to Bath from Trowbridge bus station and one travelled from Bath to Trowbridge bus station, which often arrived at Winsley at approximately the same time. If the traffic was holding them up, one waited for the other on a quiet part of the road. The one from Bath would stop at the Wheatsheaf where the road was wider, if the other one from Trowbridge was coming through late, to let the other bus come through. Occasionally the driver on the bus from Bath would get impatient and start to drive through the village and sometimes this would cause him to meet the other one also driving through the other way. The villagers got used to this happening though and the bus coming through towards Bath had to back along the road to the first turning on the right, towards the bowling green. I used to admire the way the conductors would instruct the drivers whilst they backed up to the turning.

Hooray, the other bus could pass and everything could go back to normal. (It didn't happen too many times, but we were all pleased when the bypass was built!)

The buses travelling through Winsley were double-deckers and the shooting on the roof of the Seven Stars was continuously being dislodged and broken when the bus stopped outside the pub to let people on and off the bus. Single-deckers were eventually introduced.

I remember when I used to catch the bus to get to school, I was forever running out from the pub yard to catch the bus clutching a piece of toast in one hand and a heavy satchel slung over my shoulder. The bus drivers were very good and always waited for me to jump onto the bus. "'Bout time you got up a bit earlier, Missy," they would shout.

Some wartime memories

We had an amazing cellar at the pub and I used to go down there and there would be pheasants hanging, rabbits, eggs that Mum had preserved in isinglass in old stone jars. Mum used to do wonderful preserves, using the produce from our garden. We were very, very lucky as regards food because 'Dig for Victory' was in and everyone went crazy. If you had a little bit of land you used it for growing your veggies. We had such a large garden that we used to have a chap in the village come to help look after it. During the war time, Mum used to share out some of the produce amongst the villagers.

A snippet of information gathered from some of the

No. 3 PLATOON, "B" COMPANY, 4th Bn. WILTS HOME GUARD

No. 3 Platoon, "B" Company, 4th Bn. Wiltshire Home Guard, gathered for a photoshoot outside Winsley Manor

people still living in the 'old Winsley' – apparently, the chaps from the Winsley Home Guard would occasionally meet in the Cricket Pavilion and have a general chat about the Home Guard and what other things of interest had been going on in the village – cricket matches played during the season, for instance – and always finishing up with a cup of tea. Alas on this particular evening, no one had remembered to bring the milk. Never mind – the cows belonging to 'The Chase', a very beautiful house down the lane, were grazing in the field just over the lane, probably not milked yet. Percy Hazel, who worked at The Chase, looking after the cattle, was also a member of the Home Guard but was not at the meeting. They thought he wouldn't mind if we milked them for him and used some of the milk for their cuppas (cups of tea). One can imagine Percy's astonishment when he went to milk them to find not a drop of milk was forthcoming. He must have stood for quite a while in the field scratching his head, trying to think who had done 'the milking'. All turned out all right in the end, so I'm passing this tale on to you.

I thought it an hilarious little story. It was the vision I had after listening to it of Percy standing in the field, hand on hip, scratching his head and muttering "What the bloody hell has gone on here?"

The Land Girls were there, of course. I remember that. And I just remember wonderful haymaking times, though sadly now there aren't so many fields left where haymaking takes place. We didn't have any shelter from bombs at the Seven Stars. Dad would stay in bed and Mum and I would get under the kitchen table.

My main memory, which I'm quite ashamed to say, because I didn't know much about aeroplanes and bombs, was of these Americans driving into the yard in their jeeps and coming and joining in with the villagers in the evening when the pub opened. Then this gorgeous orange suitcase would come out with all the goodies of which Mum used to share amongst some of the people who came into the pub, including me. I hardly ever had chocolates but those 'Ruth' bars – oh, what a treat! One American was called Harley and he would have supper with us. The Americans were based at the Barracks in Frome Road, Trowbridge, and they visited The Seven Stars quite frequently. I think they liked mixing with the villagers. It was not far to come in their jeeps. The locals enjoyed their company too.

Dispatch riders, with father to the left, in formation outside the former swimming baths in Bradford-on-Avon; Lamb Mill and Swan Hotel in background.

The Sanatorium

The Winsley Sanatorium was on the side of the hill coming out of the village: a collection of chalets where the patients slept. These were mostly soldiers who were suffering from consumption. I remember they wore blue pyjamas. They spent as much time as they could sitting outside on the verandahs when the weather was warm enough.

Fresh air was very good for the patients, especially the air at Winsley Hill near the Sanatorium, looking down over the valley.

I belonged to a dancing group run by the Page family who lived in the village. We visited the 'Sanny' (as it was nicknamed) and gave little shows to entertain the patients. When I was about eight, I remember especially practising for a show that involved the actors and dancers dressing up in clothes for a dancing scene. I had a grass skirt and a chiffon scarf across my top. I had borrowed this lovely scarf from my Mum but, as I danced, the scarf fell off and I was so embarrassed, left standing half-naked. I ran off the 'set' crying, because being naked around my chest was dreadful.

Boarding school and my undoing – the bar of chocolate

In 1943 I went to my first school in Trowbridge, St John's Roman Catholic School in Wingfield Road. I liked the nuns who taught there, with the exception of one. She seemed to enjoy hitting across the knuckles without good reason. The Mother Superior, Sister Cecilia, was lovely, kind and understanding, but at the same time very strict. I stayed there until I was nine years old. As the years went by, my grandparents eventually bought a house in Trowbridge and moved there, and Mum and Dad stayed on in the pub. Things did not turn out very well. Incidents happened of which you will learn later. Dad decided that

I needed to get away from the pub life for a while and get me away from troubles at home, and so packed me off to St Hilda's boarding school in Somerset. Meanwhile, my brother had been born. Mum used to bring him to school to see me. Sports Day was one occasion he came.

Dad liked to 'show off' now and then and, when the time was getting near for me to go to St. Hilda's and catch the train from Bath Station, along with other pupils living in that area, he would ask Mr Kettlety (the Chauffeur at Winsley House) to pop on his uniform (cap and all) and take me in the very posh car he drove to Bath Station. He knew the other pupils would be driven to the station in lovely cars and did not want the car I would be arriving in to be less impressive. (Gosh, what a snob!)

The train journey was always fun – we would sing songs to the rhythm of the train's engine, play cards, walk up and down the corridor, stopping to talk to the other pupils on the train, sometimes pulling down the leather straps on the windows and taking a look out – not for very long as the sooty smuts would get in our eyes and besides, the prefects on board would patrol the corridors, checking to see if we were behaving ourselves.

I was getting on quite well with my studies, improving in my piano playing and making new friends, who I eventually realised were very rich. When it came time for them to open their parcels that came in the post, we were invited to watch all the lovely goodies they had been sent. I only had one parcel all the time I was at St Hilda's. I told everyone that my parents were too busy to send parcels.

After realising that I hardly had any post from home,

some of the girls, in the same dormitory as I was, began teasing me about it... "why don't you have parcels like the rest of us? Is it because your parents aren't very rich and why don't you have many Sunday dresses to wear?" (At weekends the boarders were allowed to wear their own clothes that they brought from home)...always comments about what I didn't have, and so it went on...

Then one evening when we were getting washed and changed for supper, I couldn't find any of the clothes I had laid out on my bed to change in to. I asked the girls in the dormitory what they had done with them. They just laughed, so I knew they had done something with them, hidden them somewhere. There was nothing I could do. Then the gong sounded to summon us to go to the dining rooms. If we were late for supper we were in trouble.

I was really getting fed up with all this bullying that was going on. I grabbed a blanket from my bed, wrapped myself in it and went downstairs to the dining hall. I walked to the top table where all the teachers were sitting and shouted at them, telling them what had been going on. The girls were punished and privileges taken away. I thought I would be in trouble too for going into the hall in such a state, but no, nothing was said to me at that moment, but from then on the girls were very nice to me.

But eventually, I got so envious of all the lovely food they were sent that I watched where their tuck lockers were and, before one girl locked her locker up, I took a chocolate bar out and eventually ate it. (I'd never done anything like it before.) Unfortunately, another girl saw me remove this chocolate bar and told the Headmistress.

The next morning at assembly, it was announced that, owing to what I had done, Marilyn Elms was not to be Head Girl next term and would be leaving St Hilda's later that day. I can't remember how I got home but I know I was so ashamed of myself and that I had missed out on the opportunity of a wonderful experience – Head Girl at St Hilda's. Wow, what were Mum and Dad going to say? What would happen now? But very strangely, I felt excited and happy too. I was going to be back at the pub to be with Terry and Mum and Dad, and all my friends in the village.

Family break-up

From that time on, my life changed. Things didn't go well at the pub for Mum and Dad.

Dad started to bet on the horses and the winners were not being backed so frequently. Actually, thinking about it, probably the betting had been going on for a long time.

Mum was unhappy. Not much of a life for her. She tried so hard to take us on a few days holiday in the summer. Weymouth, in a caravan, was the usual place to go and, do you know, we really enjoyed those short breaks. Sometimes my cousins managed to be there at the same time and that was lovely.

Holidays over, Mum was back to serving behind the bar, scrubbing the floors, cleaning the windows, tending to the fires when needed, preparing food for the lunch time customers, making sure my brother was OK. I was at a new school now, St John's RC School, 'Dulce Domum', for senior pupils, in Trowbridge, and also taking evening classes at the Victoria Institute in the town centre, trying to improve my French, and taking shorthand and typing classes at Mrs Waysen's along Wingfield Road.

Unfortunately, a very sad thing happened to me when I was still at the school. Mum became very fed up with her life there at the pub. Dad was always very busy. Living in a pub, the landlord got involved in almost everything that went on in the village, organising darts matches, playing bowls for Winsley, playing skittles in the skittle alley in the Reading Rooms, arranging various coach trips to London to see the shows, as well as working at the local printers – Dotesios.

Dad seemed to be more interested in his customers rather than Mum. Obviously, yes of course, keeping the customers happy was our 'bread and butter', so to speak, but having said that, Mum wasn't getting much attention at all. As for Mum, she was not able to go to any of these functions as someone had to look after the pub. Luckily, when my father could look after the pub, as she was able to drive and had her own car, she would drive off to visit various relations and friends, usually at Farleigh Wick.

Well, eventually Mum left the Seven Stars. While things had been difficult, she had been befriended by a painter and decorator who had been working in the village and spent his lunch breaks in the Tap Room, and she had been seeing him whenever she could. I can't ever remember seeing him in the pub at all. A lot of these meetings must have been going on for a long time, probably while I was away at school.

I personally did not realise what was happening until one day at school. I was sat in the school hall, taking my school certificate exams, when the Mother Superior, Sister Cecelia, came up to me where I was sitting (I remember hearing her words so clearly), "Marilyn, something sad has happened. Your mummy has gone away and left Terence with your daddy, so you will have to go home and look after your brother until further arrangements can be made. There is a car outside waiting to take you home". Dad had arranged for the car from Winsley House to collect me and take me home to the pub.

A day I shall never forget, Dad was in shock and Terry kept holding my hand and saying "Marilyn, where has Mummy gone?" Well, as you can imagine, I thought how could I explain everything to my darling brother and how would we all manage? I was twelve years old and my brother two. Dad was so upset wondering how we were going to manage.

Life was pretty horrible for a very long time, but the villagers were wonderful. Dad, unbeknown to me, had spent a fortune on the horses and got himself into debt with the Brewery, the local village shops and well, with pretty much everyone.

There was no money for food. To help, I used to take my money box to the Post Office/grocery shop and take out what I could. I did the same with my Post Office savings book. I had saved a little in there with the pocket money from Granny and Grampy.

Soon, all my savings had gone. The only places where I might get some help were the two shops in the village.

The Post Office/grocery shop was the first one I went to. I had to ask Mr and Mrs Gerrish if they could let me have some bits and pieces for our evening meal. Then, the next day, I would go to the Wheatsheaf and ask the same. I was so embarrassed. They knew the situation and were very good – as often happened in country villages. Everyone 'mucked in' and, as the saying goes, 'absolutely marvellous'.

Soon after this was happening, the Brewery gave Dad a warning that he would no longer be landlord of the Seven Stars as his debts had ruined the business. An auction was arranged for Dad to sell most of our possessions. He kept back a few items for us to keep. The auction took place in the Club Room upstairs.

I was out at the time and did not know that it was happening. When I got home pretty well everything had gone. Nearly everything we had was sold; sadly, lots of things were bought by the villagers. Terry's toys had gone including his favourite pink teddy, as had all my personal belongings. What a situation! Almost everything was gone and soon there would be no home. How I got through the following weeks and months I'll never know. My main concern was my darling brother, Terry. What could I tell him when he used to find my hand and tug it and say those awful words, "Marilyn, where has my Mummy gone?" My mind from those days went quite bananas with worry.

Dad tried everywhere to get somewhere to live. He made contact with just about everyone he knew to see if they could put him, Terry and me up, until we could find something more permanent. In the end, Dotesios let us move into some rooms above the office which had been redecorated and had two bedrooms, a bathroom and a kitchen. It was very damp and we had regular visits from the river rats. The building is still there and lived in. I believe there is a plaque on the wall further down the road stating that these flats belong to Dotesios, the printers.

Now, getting back to the river rats, I remember the first Easter we were there. I had filled a carrier bag with Easter eggs for my brother and hid them in my bedroom for Terry to come in and get them on Easter Day morning. He came in and got into bed with me. As I retrieved the bag form under the bed and opened it, out scrambled two or three rats. My brother didn't seem too upset as the eggs inside were still intact. I think I was the one most upset. Well, that was that.

Dad went off looking for somewhere else to live and eventually found somewhere in a lovely big house along the Trowbridge Road in Bradford-on-Avon, with a business colleague, Mr Salter and his wife. They had no children and let us have rooms. Dad and Terry shared a bed and I had a small bedroom further up in the attic. Luckily, Dad still had his job at Dotesios at Greenland Mills, so had the rent money.

Unfortunately, Mrs Salter took an instant liking to Terry and wanted to adopt him. This caused us great upsets and we had to make plans to move again. Luckily, a council house became available and, because of our situation, we were offered it. Once again, so many of the villagers helped us move and settle in at 10 Danes Rise, Winsley.

This was near the beginning of development of the farmland, Bowles farming land – haymaking fields gone.

My Mum's brother, Uncle David and Aunty Tessa lived just down the road and they helped me make curtains and gave us all sorts of things for the house such as china and bed linen. They had no children so were only too pleased to help out. They were wonderful people. Bless them, they gave me the strength to carry on.

I used to spend a lot of time with them in later years. By then, I had a car and used to take my Aunty to her favourite place to go – a garden centre. They had a lovely garden. I remember that every time we went to get her plants, she always bought me one too.

During this time, eventually Mum got in touch to tell me where she was. She was applying for a job on the buses as a conductress. She was living with Frank (the painter and decorator). Arrangements were made to meet up with Mum on a regular basis. This was very often at the Gaumont Cinema in Trowbridge. My brother loved the pictures and then, afterwards, we would go to the Penguin fish and chip shop and walk around the town eating our fish and chips, then off back home on the bus.

Dad was lonely and missed the pub life so much that he used to entertain a few of his old friends and lady customers at home. This was not a good experience for me, preparing them bread and cheese with Dad providing the drinks. Then the gramophone was put on and Dad used to say "Go and have a dance Marilyn". By this time, all of his friends were a bit 'merry'. I didn't enjoy those evenings at all. All the time my brother was asleep upstairs.

Nothing wrong ever happened but I hated those evenings.

Some of them visited our house frequently, including one lady called Jean. She had a family of two girls and two boys, very well travelled and eventually lived at 10 Danes Rise. I actually got on very well with Jean and her family. She eventually married Dad and moved to Bath. The children went their own ways.

My brother Terence, or Terry as he was generally known, I think was rather bewildered with what was going on and sometimes would ring me at home after I was married. He would say that he wasn't very happy and could he come and stay a while. He did, then went back to Winsley. Soon after he got a job at Dotesios and got friendly with a girl called Jean who he married on 24th July 1965.

Going to work

At Danes Rise, the time came for me to think of going out to work. Dad always wanted me to join Lloyds Bank. He banked in Bradford-on-Avon and I always remember going with him to pay in the takings. The Bank Manager, Mr James, would always come out to meet him. I tried to get a job at Lloyds in Trowbridge but didn't have the exam results to prove I would be suitable for a banking career.

Anyway, I wrote to Mr Ingamells, the then Bank Manager in Trowbridge, explaining the situation and that I would be prepared to work for nothing if he would give me a trial period. After a couple of interviews, I think he was surprised at my approach – a bit different and not at all the right way to go about things. However, a few weeks later a letter came through the post saying it had been agreed by Head Office and Mr Ingamells that I could go on a six months trial with an appropriate salary. Hooray! It's good to be a bit cheeky sometimes.

I was kept on as an office junior and stayed there for quite a few years. I loved the work, eventually serving on the counter. I was moved to the Bradford-on-Avon Branch, as an employee at Bradford wanted to transfer to Trowbridge, so we did a swap. I loved my time in the Bank, meeting all the different customers. I still see a lot of the customers now. Bradford people didn't move very far away – neither did the village people at the top of the hill – Winsley, and the people living in all the little hamlets.

Marrying

Meanwhile I met my future husband, Peter Maundrell. It was the uniform which first caused me to wonder who this rather handsome young man was walking along Bridge Street, probably on his way to a Royal Observer Corps meeting nearby. The uniform he was wearing was Air Force Blue in colour; his cap folded in his epaulette on the shoulder. He used to tell me that joining the ROC was the next best thing to joining the Air Force. This, he had intended to do from a very early age, but due to ill-health, he failed the medical.

Mr Pymont from Conkwell (Chief Observer), and the Head Gardener at Belcombe Court, Mr Swain (Leading

Observer), had encouraged Peter to join. The original observation post was in a field in Budbury in Bradford-on-Avon, when the task was to detect enemy bombers. Then, at the start of the Cold War, a bunker was built in a field in the lanes at Ashley. The ROC posts were built with the purpose of monitoring nuclear fallout. Two or three observers were usually on duty at the same time about once a month.

Several bunkers were built around the area, being named Charlie 1, 2, 3 and 4. No. 4 was the Bradford-on-Avon post. The group had meetings occasionally at different venues and 'speakers' were invited to go and give talks on various aspects of the ROC.

Peter stayed with the ROC for a long time and became a Leading Observer. He was presented with a long service medal which was for twelve years' service but actually he stayed with them for fourteen years.

We got married at St Nicholas's Church on 10th June, 1961, and had a reception in the Winsley village hall. Initially, Peter and I lived with his parents in their house in Bradford-on-Avon. This was a wonderful house in St Margaret's Place, with a big garden, cats and dogs and lovely neighbours. I left the bank a few years later.

I had a daughter, Lesley, in Berryfield Maternity Hospital, and Peter and I have lived in Bradford-on-Avon until the present day.

Missing Winsley

Peter was born and bred in Bradford-on-Avon and glad to be settled here. I missed Winsley and still do.